Financial Freedom Roadmap:

A Step-by-Step Guide to Building Wealth

Copyright Contents

Table of Content

Chapter 1: "Understanding Financial Freedom"

Understanding financial freedom is the first step in realizing your ambitions of a life free of money-related stress and limits in a society where financial stability and independence are highly valued. We will go deeply into the notion of financial freedom, study its importance, evaluate the many pathways one may take to reach it and aid you in defining clear financial goals and objectives to begin your journey toward financial independence.

Defining Financial Independence

Financial independence means many things to different individuals, but at its heart, it refers to the capacity to make life decisions without being excessively concerned about the financial implications. It implies having the ability to follow your interests, make choices based on what you value most, and live life on your terms, rather than being constrained by financial or resource constraints.

For others, financial independence may imply the capacity to retire early and live a comfortable life without working. Others may consider it to be the ability to travel the globe, establish a company, or spend more time with loved ones. Finally, it comes down to having the financial resources to do what you want, when you want, and without having to worry about money.

The Importance of Financial Independence

Financial independence is important for various reasons:

Reduced Stress: Financial independence means having fewer anxieties about paying bills, managing daily costs, or coping with unanticipated financial crises. It alleviates tension, which may hurt your general well-being.

Increased Flexibility: Financial freedom allows you to make decisions based on your principles and aspirations. You may take sensible chances, investigate new possibilities, and gain more control over your life.

Wealth Creation: Financial independence often leads to wealth accumulation. When you no longer have to live paycheck to paycheck, you can devote more resources to investments and wealth-building activities.

Financial independence allows you to prepare for retirement on your terms. You may retire early if that's your desire, or work longer if you like what you do and don't have to worry about money.

Pursuing Your Passions: Financial independence allows you to pursue your hobbies and passions. Whether you want to travel the globe, join a charity, or pursue artistic activities, financial stability makes these goals attainable.

Improved Quality of Life: Financial independence is often associated with improved quality of life. It enables you to enjoy experiences and possibilities that were previously beyond of reach, like better healthcare and a more comfortable house.

Family and Community: Financial independence is about more than just personal prosperity. It may also have a good influence on your family and community. It allows you to help loved ones, donate to charity organizations, and leave a financial legacy for future generations.

Reduced Fear of the Unknown: Financially independent Individuals are better prepared to confront unforeseen problems, such as a health crisis, job loss, or economic slump. This minimizes anxiety about the unknown and improves mental health.

Establishing Specific Financial Goals and Objectives

Financial independence does not come by accident; it is the consequence of diligent preparation and goal setting. Consider the following steps to establish clear financial goals and objectives:

Define Your "Why": Determine why you desire financial independence. What are your hopes, desires, and plans for the future?

Examine Your Current Financial Situation: Examine your current financial situation, including your income, spending, assets, and obligations. This evaluation will serve as the basis for developing your objectives.

Set SMART objectives: Specific, Measurable, Achievable, Relevant, and Time-bound goals (SMART). Let's say, for instance, "I want to save $10,000 in an emergency fund within the next 12 months."

Prioritize Your Objectives: Not all objectives are equal in value. Determine which objectives are the most important and need your immediate attention.

Make a plan of action: Define the steps needed to accomplish each objective. What steps will you take to achieve financial independence?

Track Your Progress: Monitor your progress regularly, alter your objectives as appropriate, and enjoy your victories along the way.

Entrepreneurship: If you're interested in starting your own business, keep in mind that it sometimes requires risk-taking and uncertainty. Successful entrepreneurs are resilient and adaptive. They find and fill market gaps. Building a company from the ground up may be very rewarding, but it demands tenacity and devotion.

Passive income sources are essential components of many people's financial emancipation journeys. Income through investments, rental properties, or royalties, for example, might give financial security even while you are not actively working. Building them requires an initial commitment of time or money, and they often develop steadily over time.

Job Advancement: Investing in education and skill development is critical for people seeking financial independence via a job. Identifying growth chances and networking may help you climb the corporate ladder or get access to higher-paying professions. Remember that maintaining a work-life balance is critical on this road.

Frugality: A thrifty lifestyle may be an effective technique for saving and building money. You may dedicate more of your income to savings and investing by cutting needless costs and living within your means. It is about making deliberate decisions to spend your money on what is genuinely important to you.

Visualize Your Objectives: In addition to articulating your "why," spend time visualizing your objectives. Make a vision board or write a thorough description of your life when you've attained financial independence. Visualization may be a very effective motivator.

Maintain Your Commitment: Financial independence is a process that demands perseverance. There may be challenges and disappointments, but keeping focused on your objectives and learning from your mistakes is essential. Accept setbacks as chances to learn and increase your financial awareness.

Financial independence is a very personal aim. It's about living a life that reflects your beliefs and goals. You're well on your way to accumulating wealth and ensuring the future you want by recognizing its importance, researching the many routes to achieving it, and making clear, achievable financial objectives. In the next parts of this ebook, we will give step-by-step instructions on how to make your dreams a reality.

Chapter 2: "Creating a Solid Financial Foundation"

Creating a sound financial foundation is analogous to constructing the cornerstone of a robust structure on the path to financial independence. This chapter is devoted to assisting you in laying that cornerstone. We'll discuss the necessity of having an emergency fund, tactics for efficiently managing and lowering debt, and advice on creating a budget and monitoring costs. These crucial actions will not only increase your financial stability but will also put you on the road to wealth-building and peace of mind.

Putting Money Aside for Unexpected Expenses

Life is full of unexpected events, not all of them are pleasant. Medical problems, auto repairs, or unexpected job loss may all occur at any time. These catastrophes might upset your financial condition if you don't have a safety net. This is when an emergency fund comes in handy.

What exactly is an emergency fund?

An emergency fund is a special savings account set up to address unexpected financial problems. It serves as your financial safety net, ensuring that you can manage unforeseen costs without going into debt or jeopardizing your long-term financial objectives.

Why is an emergency fund necessary?

Financial stability is provided by an emergency fund, which reduces worry and stress amid unexpected financial losses.

Avoiding Debt: Having an emergency fund allows you to meet expenditures without relying on credit cards or loans, which sometimes have high-interest rates.

Long-Term Goal Preservation: It keeps you from having to tap into your long-term assets or retirement funds when unforeseen expenditures occur.

Building an Emergency Fund:

Establish a Goal: Decide how much money you want in your emergency fund. Many financial gurus advise saving three to six months of living costs.

Create an automated transfer from your checking account to a second savings account. Consider this a non-negotiable monthly cost.

Start Small: If you can't save the whole amount advised at first, set a lower target and gradually raise it.

Windfalls: Put unexpected financial windfalls, such as tax returns or job bonuses, into your emergency fund.

Prioritize Your Reserve: Prioritize your emergency reserve before aggressive debt reduction or long-term investments.

Keep it Liquid: For your emergency fund, choose a high-yield savings account or a money market account. When necessary, these accounts are conveniently accessible.

Effective Debt Management and Reduction

Debt, if not handled appropriately, maybe a significant impediment to financial independence. This part will teach you how to manage and minimize your debts successfully.

Understanding the Different Types of Debt:

Good Debt: Some debts, such as a house mortgage or student loans for education, are deemed "good" since they assist in creating assets or boosting earning potential.

hefty-interest debts, such as credit card balances and payday loans, are often seen as "bad" since they frequently result in financial hardship and hefty interest charges.

Debt Management that Works:

Make a debt inventory, which includes the kind of debt, outstanding amount, interest rate, and minimum monthly payments.

Prioritize High-Interest Debt: Pay off your highest-interest obligations first. Allocate more funds to these debts while paying the bare minimum on others.

Budget Wisely: Create a budget that permits you to make regular debt payments while still keeping your emergency fund and other financial objectives in mind.

Negotiate Interest Rates: Contact your creditors to discuss lowering your interest rates, particularly if you have a strong payment history.

Debt consolidation is combining various loans into a single, lower-interest loan, making payments more feasible.

Snowball vs. Avalanche: Select the best debt repayment approach for you. The "avalanche" strategy reduces interest expenses by focusing on high-interest rate loans, while the "snowball" method prioritizes smaller debts for quick wins.

Avoid Taking on New Debt: When feasible, avoid taking on new debt while paying off current debt. This assists you in breaking the debt-accumulating loop.

Making a Budget and Keeping Track of Expenses

A well-structured budget serves as your financial GPS, directing you to your financial objectives. In this part, we'll go through how to make a budget and how to keep track of your costs.

Making a Budget:

Determine Your Income: Determine your monthly income, taking into account your salary, side hustle revenue, and any other sources of money.

Make a list of your expenses: Organize all of your monthly costs into fixed (e.g., rent, mortgage, utilities) and variable (e.g., food, entertainment).

Establish Financial Objectives: Determine your financial objectives, such as saving for a trip, paying off debt, or creating an emergency fund.

Make a budget that assigns a part of your money to each spending area and your financial objectives.

Monitor and Adjust: Review your budget regularly and make adjustments as required to remain on target.

Keeping Track of Expenses:

Keep Track of All Spending: Keep track of all expenditures, no matter how minor. Apps, spreadsheets, or good old-fashioned pen and paper may all be used.

Categorize spending: For simple analysis, group your spending into categories (e.g., groceries, transportation, and entertainment).

Analyze Your Spending: Review your costs regularly to find areas where you may cut down or reallocate funds to better fit with your objectives.

Avoid impulsive Spending: Before making an impulsive buy, assess if it is in line with your budget and financial goals.

Building a sound financial foundation is a critical step toward financial independence. By creating an emergency fund, efficiently managing and lowering debt, and creating a budget to monitor costs, you are laying the financial framework for pursuing your objectives and achieving long-term financial stability. In the following chapters, we will go further into numerous financial techniques and tools to help you strengthen your financial foundation and lead you toward your ultimate financial objectives.

In the next parts of this chapter, we will look at the art of diversifying your investment portfolio as well as tactics for successful investing, to help you make educated choices to generate long-term wealth while efficiently managing risk.

Chapter 3: "Investing for Long-Term Wealth"

Introduction to Different Investment Options (Stocks, Real Estate, Bonds, and so on)

Investing is the foundation of long-term wealth creation. In this chapter, we'll take a look at the world of investments, looking at a variety of alternatives such as stocks, real estate, bonds, and more. We'll go over their distinct qualities, possible benefits, and how to get started on your journey to increasing your wealth via wise and educated investing decisions.

Understanding the Fundamentals of Investing

Before we get into particular investment possibilities, it's important to understand certain basic ideas that apply to all forms of investments:

Risk and Return: Risk and return are inextricably linked in the world of investment. Generally, investments with bigger potential returns are riskier. The appropriate balance is determined by your risk tolerance, financial objectives, and time horizon.

Diversification: Spreading your assets across many asset types reduces risk. Diversification may improve portfolio stability by reducing the effect of a poor-performing asset on total returns.

Liquidity: The ease with which an investment may be turned into cash without suffering a major loss in value. Stocks and bonds are more liquid than real estate and other alternative assets.

Time Horizon: The amount of time you want to invest is referred to as your time horizon. Because you can survive short-term market volatility, a longer time horizon generally permits you to take on greater risk.

Let us now look at some of the most popular investing options:

1. Securities

Stocks reflect a company's ownership. When you purchase a share of stock, you become a shareholder and have access to the company's earnings (or losses) as well as voting rights. Here's everything you need to know:

Stocks offer the potential for significant long-term growth, making them appealing to investors trying to accumulate wealth over time.

Stock values may be erratic, and individual corporations may encounter financial difficulties or downturns. Diversification across several equities may aid in mitigating these risks.

How to Invest: You may purchase stocks via a brokerage account, which gives you access to stock exchanges such as the New York Stock Exchange (NYSE) and the NASDAQ.

2. Actual Estate

Real estate investing includes purchasing, owning, and sometimes managing properties. Real estate may give both rental income and the possibility of capital gain. The following are some essential points:

Passive Income: Rental assets in real estate may create passive income. It is extremely popular among individuals looking for cash flow.

Real estate assets may appreciate over time, possibly resulting in cash profits when sold.

Risks: Real estate investments may be costly in terms of money and may need continuous upkeep and administration. Property prices are also influenced by market circumstances.

How to Invest: You may buy real estate directly or indirectly via real estate investment trusts (REITs) or real estate crowdfunding platforms.

3. Bonds

Debt instruments issued by governments, municipalities, or businesses are known as bonds. When you buy bonds, you are effectively lending money to the issuer in exchange for periodic interest payments and the return of the principal amount when the bond matures:

Bonds provide consistent interest payments, making them suitable for investors looking for stability and income.

High-quality bonds, such as US Treasury bonds, are regarded as reasonably secure investments. Lower-quality bonds, on the other hand, are riskier.

Risks: Changes in interest rates may cause bond values to fall, and lower-quality bonds may default.

Bonds may be purchased directly from the issuer or via bond mutual funds and exchange-traded funds (ETFs).

4. Mutual funds and exchange-traded funds

Mutual funds and exchange-traded funds (ETFs) aggregate money from different participants to invest in a diverse portfolio of stocks, bonds, and other assets:

Diversification: Mutual funds and exchange-traded funds (ETFs) provide quick diversification by distributing risk across a variety of assets.

Professional Management: Professional portfolio managers handle these funds and make investment choices on your behalf.

Liquidity: Mutual funds and ETFs offer liquidity since you can readily purchase and sell shares.

How to Invest: Mutual funds and ETFs may be purchased via brokerage accounts.

5. Diversified Investments

Alternative investments include hedge funds, private equity, venture capital, commodities, and other non-traditional assets:

Diversification: Alternative investments might help to diversify a portfolio and perhaps minimize risk.

Complexity: These investments may be difficult to understand and may need a greater degree of knowledge.

Some alternative investments, such as private equity and hedge funds, may have low liquidity.

How to Invest: Access to alternative investments varies, and it is generally necessary to be an authorized investor.

You may be wondering, now that you've been exposed to these many investing alternatives, which is the best option for you. The answer is determined by your financial objectives, risk tolerance, and investment horizon.

Chapter 4: "Income Generation Strategies"

Income creation is a critical component of your financial journey, and it extends beyond the confines of a single paycheck from your employment. This chapter offers an exploring journey through the several alternatives for generating various streams of income, such as side hustles, investments, and passive income. It goes deeply into these varied sources of income, assists you in discovering chances to supplement your main income, and offers useful insights and ideas for developing a sustainable and broad income portfolio. By the conclusion of this chapter, you will have the knowledge you need to confidently manage your financial journey and safeguard your financial future.

Investigating Multiple Income Streams

The concept of depending only on one source of income has grown increasingly outmoded. To maintain financial stability and security in our ever-changing economy, it is critical to investigate several sources of income. Here are some options to consider:

1. Side Business

Side hustles, which were formerly considered new, are now an important source of revenue. These activities might include freelance employment, product sales, or service providing in addition to your principal job. It is important to understand the distinctions of side hustles:

Side hustles are well-known for their adaptability. They enable you to work on your own schedule, making them an excellent solution for individuals who have a full-time job or other obligations.

Diverse Opportunities: You may personalize your side hustle to match your interests, abilities, or hobbies, making it more entertaining and even profitable.

Earning Potential: The earning potential of side hustles varies greatly. Some may provide a little supplemental income, while others may grow into full-fledged enterprises.

Steps to Get Started: To guarantee that your side hustle is satisfying and sustainable, you must do research, estimate earning possibilities, and develop a complete strategy.

2. Investing

Investing is a tried-and-true way to build money over time. Investments sometimes require an initial financial investment, but they also provide the possibility of producing passive income. Here are some of the most important investing possibilities to consider:

Individual stocks or diversified funds may provide dividend income as well as possible capital gains. Stocks are well-known for their long-term growth potential.

Real estate investments include owning rental properties as well as investing in real estate investment trusts (REITs). These investments may provide rental income as well as property appreciation.

Bonds are debt instruments issued by governments, municipalities, or businesses. They provide interest, which provides a consistent source of income, particularly for risk-averse investors.

Mutual funds and exchange-traded funds (ETFs) aggregate money from different individuals to invest in diverse portfolios of stocks, bonds, or other assets.

Steps to Get Started: To begin your investing journey, do thorough research into the various investment possibilities, analyze your risk tolerance, and maybe seek help from a financial adviser or use online investment platforms to implement your investment plan.

3. Earnings from a Passive Source

Passive income is money that works for you while you are sleeping. It entails generating money with little to no active participation. The following are examples of common passive income sources:

Dividend Stocks: Investing in dividend-paying firms may offer a constant source of passive income.

Royalties: You may earn royalties from your creative works if you are a writer, musician, or content provider.

Online companies: Online companies that are automated, such as e-commerce sites or affiliate marketing, may provide passive revenue.

Crowdfunding for Real Estate: Crowdfunding platforms allow you to invest in real estate projects and earn passive rental income.

How to Get Started: Creating content, developing a company, or acquiring assets all require significant initial work to generate passive income streams. The idea is to design systems that need as little continuous input as possible.

Discovering Opportunities to Increase Your Primary Income

While it is critical to diversify your income via numerous sources, your principal source of income remains a cornerstone in your financial path. Here's how to identify possibilities to increase your main income:

Assess Your Existing Skills and Credentials: Begin by examining your current skills and credentials. Examine if your present position or sector offers prospects for career progression, skill improvement, or pay negotiation.

Consider extending your education or learning more abilities to supplement your skill set. Education and training may lead to higher-paying jobs or whole new career pathways.

Job Market Research: Conduct market research to find sectors or occupations with high earning potential. Certain industries pay more and provide more employment stability.

Building a strong professional network may lead to new career possibilities, promotions, and a better awareness of business trends. Attend industry events, participate in online groups, and cultivate connections with coworkers and mentors.

Side Projects: If your abilities and interests overlap, consider starting side projects or entrepreneurial activities that might grow into principal revenue sources in the future.

Tips for Creating a Long-Term Income Strategy

Building a sustainable income plan requires more than just increasing your wages; it also entails maintaining a good work-life balance and assuring long-term financial stability. Here are some pointers to help you:

Set Specific Financial Goals: Clearly outline your financial goals, whether they be to pay off debt, save for a property, or retire comfortably. Your revenue approach will be guided by well-defined targets.

Diversify Your Income: Avoid the dangers of depending on a single source of income. Multiple revenue sources give stability and resilience, protecting you from unanticipated financial upheavals.

Spend Your Money Wisely: Create a budget that reflects your financial goals and income. Monitor your spending and savings carefully to verify that your financial resources are being used wisely.

Invest for the Long Run: Investing is a fundamental aspect of wealth growth. Whether you're investing in stocks, real estate, or other assets, be sure your investments are in line with your long-term goals.

Stay current on industry developments by investing in continuing education and skill development. This not only keeps you competitive in the labor market but also increases your earning potential.

Work-Life Balance: While increasing your money is necessary, don't sacrifice your health or personal life to achieve financial success. A sustainable income plan considers your total well-being.

Risk management entails being prepared for financial setbacks such as job loss, economic downturns, or unanticipated costs. Building an emergency fund is an important part of risk management.

Seek Professional Help: If you find yourself in a new area with your income plan or investments, consider consulting with a knowledgeable financial counselor or consultant.

Remember that developing a good income plan is a journey that involves a careful balance of hard effort, continual learning, and adaptation. You are well-equipped to build a solid foundation for financial success by examining numerous revenue sources, discovering possibilities to increase your main income, and following these guidelines. The next chapters will go into more tactics and resources to help you turn your financial dreams into reality.

In the next chapters, we will continue to look at other financial strategies, methods, and tools to help you reach your financial goals, whether they be to save for retirement, develop wealth, or attain financial independence.

Chapter 5: "Financial Planning and Goal Setting"

Financial planning and goal setting are navigational tools that help you map your path to financial success. This chapter will guide you through the process of building a detailed financial plan and schedule, as well as the critical practice of measuring your progress and making modifications as required. By the conclusion of this chapter, you'll have gained the information and skills necessary to create a clear and attainable financial plan that corresponds with your goals.

Setting SMART Financial Objectives

Setting goals is the first step in any financial planning process. However, not all objectives are created equal. To guarantee that your objectives are well-defined and reachable, make them *SMART:*

Your objectives should be clear and precise. Rather than stating, "I want to save money," say, "I want to save $10,000 for a down payment on a home."

Measurable: Your objectives should be measurable so that you can monitor your progress. "I want to pay off $5,000 in credit card debt" is a quantifiable objective.

Achievable: Your objectives should be attainable given your financial situation. While aspiring to become a billionaire is admirable, having attainable goals is critical for motivation and growth.

Relevant: Your goals should be in line with your beliefs and long-term aspirations. Make certain that they contribute to your overall financial well-being.

Time-bound: Your objectives should be time-bound. Setting a deadline instills urgency and helps you to measure your progress. Let's say for example, "I want to save $10,000 for a down payment in three years."

Goals for the Short, Mid, and Long Term

Financial objectives may be divided into three categories based on their timeframe: short-term, mid-term, and long-term.

Short-Term Goals: These normally have one year. Creating an emergency fund, paying off credit card debt, or saving for a trip are some examples.

Mid-Term Objectives: These have a one to five-year time range. Saving for a vehicle, beginning a small company, or supporting your child's education are some examples.

Long-Term Goals: These should be set for at least five years. Saving for retirement, purchasing a property, and establishing financial independence are some examples.

Making a Financial Plan and a Timeline

It's time to make a financial plan when you've defined and prioritized your objectives. Your financial plan serves as a road map, directing you toward your goals. Here's how to create a thorough financial plan:

Assess Your Present Financial Situation: To begin, determine your present financial situation. Determine your earnings, spending, assets, and liabilities. This will provide you with a clear picture of your money.

Determine which of your SMART objectives are the most significant and correspond with your beliefs. Prioritizing your objectives can help you manage your resources more efficiently.

Make a plan of action: Divide each aim into manageable stages. If you're saving for a down payment, for example, your action plan can involve cutting down on discretionary spending, looking for extra income streams, and investigating mortgage choices.

Determine how much money you need to invest in each objective and create a budget to guarantee you can achieve these financial obligations.

Establish Milestones: In addition to your overall SMART objectives, establish smaller milestones to track your progress. Milestones give you a feeling of accomplishment and keep you motivated.

Create a Timeline: Set deadlines for your objectives and achievements. A precise timeline can assist you in staying on track and making required modifications if you are lagging.

Review and adjust your financial strategy regularly. As your life circumstances change, you may need to revise your objectives or action plan.

Seek Professional Advice: If your financial position is complicated or you're unclear about specific components of your strategy, talk to a financial counselor.

Monitoring Progress and Making Adjustments to Your Plan as Needed

Setting SMART objectives, developing a financial strategy, and making a timeframe is merely the beginning of the road. Tracking your progress and changing your strategy as appropriate keeps your financial objectives within reach. Here's how to successfully track your financial progress:

Regular Reviews: Review your financial strategy and overall progress toward your objectives regularly. A quarterly or yearly review is an excellent place to start.

Expense Tracking: Keep a record of your costs. Budgeting tools and spreadsheets may be really useful in this respect.

Milestone Comparison: Compare your accomplished milestones to your original expectations. Rethink your action plan or timeframe if you're going behind.

Celebrate Your Successes: Don't forget to recognize your accomplishments. Recognizing your financial achievements is critical for keeping motivated.

Adjust as Needed: Life is fluid, and financial circumstances may change. Adapt your financial plan as needed to account for changes in income, spending, or ambitions.

Keep Up to Date: Stay up to date on economic trends, investing possibilities, and financial strategy. As you develop, this information will assist you in making educated judgments.

Seek Professional Advice: If your financial position becomes extremely complex, or if you want experience in certain areas, consider hiring a financial counselor to give assistance and suggestions.

Goal formulation and financial planning are both dynamic processes. Your strategy should adapt in response to changes in your financial condition and ambitions. The flexibility to monitor your progress and adjust your strategy is what guarantees your financial journey stays flexible, manageable, and in line with your long-term financial objectives.

Chapter 6: "Protecting and Preserving Your Wealth"

Your money is the consequence of your efforts and wise financial judgments. It's now time to safeguard and maintain what you've created. In this chapter, we'll look at asset protection and estate planning techniques, delving into insurance and risk management, and discussing the necessity of long-term financial sustainability and legacy planning. By the conclusion of this chapter, you'll know how to protect your riches and leave a lasting legacy for future generations.

Asset Protection and Estate Planning Strategies

Asset preservation and estate planning are critical components of asset management. They include protecting your assets from possible hazards and ensuring that your intentions for estate distribution are carried out properly. Consider the following major strategies:

1. Make a thorough estate plan.

Will: A will is a legal document that specifies how your assets will be transferred upon your death. It lets you name beneficiaries and guarantee that your assets are distributed how you choose.

Trusts: Trusts are adaptable estate planning strategies that may assist in safeguarding your assets from probate, decrease estate taxes, and provide for unique situations such as young children or special needs heirs.

Power of Attorney: Giving someone you trust the authority to make financial and legal choices on your behalf if you become unable to do so.

Healthcare Directive: A healthcare directive, also known as a living will or healthcare proxy, describes your medical care preferences if you are unable to make choices for yourself.

Regular Updates: Estate planning is a continuous process. As your life circumstances change, such as marriage, divorce, or the birth of a kid, review and revise your plan.

2. Asset Protection Techniques

Diversify your assets: Spreading your investments across multiple asset classes might help you reduce risk. A well-balanced portfolio can safeguard your money from the volatility of a single asset class.

Insurance: Insurance is a critical asset protection instrument. Insurance policies such as homes, vehicles, and umbrella insurance cover a variety of dangers.

Limited Liability Entities: If you own a business, you may safeguard your assets by organizing it as a limited liability company (LLC) or corporation.

FLPs are legal frameworks that enable you to manage and safeguard family assets while decreasing estate taxes. They allow you to pass assets on to future generations while maintaining control.

Pre-nuptial and post-nuptial agreements may safeguard your assets in the event of a divorce and assist in defining how property and assets will be distributed.

Understanding Risk Management and Insurance

Insurance is critical in protecting your assets and minimizing risks. Understanding different forms of insurance and risk management solutions is critical:

1. Medical Insurance

Health insurance offers financial security in the event of medical bills, as well as peace of mind and access to treatment.

Coverage Options: Learn about health insurance plans such as Health Maintenance Organizations (HMOs), Preferred Provider Organizations (PPOs), and High Deductible Health Plans

(HDHPs) with Health Savings Accounts (HSAs).

Long-Term Care Insurance: As you become older, long-term care insurance may help pay for nursing homes, assisted living facilities, or in-home care.

2. Insurance for Property and Casualty

Homeowners insurance protects your house and personal items in the event of damage or theft. High-value objects may be protected by additional riders.

Auto insurance is needed in most locations and offers financial protection in the event of an accident, damage, or theft.

Umbrella insurance provides supplementary liability coverage above and beyond the limitations of your main policies, offering an extra layer of protection.

3. Term Life Insurance

Term life insurance offers coverage for a certain period and is often less costly than permanent life insurance. It is appropriate for shielding your loved ones while you are working.

Permanent life insurance, such as whole life or universal life, provides everlasting coverage and may increase monetary value over time. It is often utilized as part of estate planning.

4. Disability Coverage

Income Replacement: Disability insurance replaces a part of your earnings if you are unable to work due to sickness or accident. It is particularly crucial for those who depend on their income to maintain their standard of living.

5. General Liability Insurance

Personal Liability Insurance: Personal liability insurance protects you if you are judged legally liable for hurting or damaging someone else's property. It may be included in your homeowners or renters insurance.

Professional Liability Insurance: If you work as a doctor, lawyer, or architect, professional liability insurance protects you against malpractice lawsuits.

Legacy Planning and Long-Term Financial Sustainability

Long-term financial sustainability and legacy planning are required to ensure your money lasts for generations. Here are some crucial points to consider:

1. Retirement Preparation

Contribute to retirement accounts such as 401(k)s and IRAs regularly to develop a nest egg for your retirement years.

Social Security: Learn how Social Security works and when you are eligible to receive it.

Investments: Continue to invest prudently, tweaking your portfolio to lower risk as you approach retirement.

2. Charitable Contributions

Consider adding charity giving into your financial strategy. Charitable contributions not only have a beneficial effect, but they may also provide tax advantages.

Donor-Advised Funds: Donor-Advised Funds enable you to donate to a charity account, get an instant tax credit, and make recommendations to your favorite organizations over time.

3. Tax-Affordable Strategies

Tax Planning: Optimize your investments and financial choices to reduce taxes, such as via tax-advantaged accounts and smart gifts.

4. Estate and Legacy Planning

Legacy Planning: Determine your desired legacy. Consider how you want to be remembered and what ideals you want future generations to inherit.

Consider generational wealth options, such as trusts or family foundations, if conserving money for your heirs is a goal.

Estate Taxes: Understand the estate tax thresholds and how they may impact your estate. Consult with an estate planning attorney to devise a tax-minimizing approach.

Communication: It is critical to have open and honest communication with your heirs about your financial legacy and ideals to ensure a seamless asset shift and wealth preservation.

5. Financial Consultants

Professional Advice: Consulting with a knowledgeable financial adviser or estate planning attorney may give helpful guidance on long-term financial sustainability and legacy planning.

Financial planning is an ongoing activity that grows in response to life's circumstances and ambitions. You may achieve long-term financial sustainability and legacy planning by adopting asset protection and estate planning, understanding insurance and risk management, and concentrating on long-term financial sustainability and legacy planning.

www.ingramcontent.com/pod-product-compliance
Lightning Source LLC
Chambersburg PA
CBHW062258290526
45794CB00006B/2604